Contents

Introduction

Developing French supports the teaching of French to beginners. It is designed for teachers and parents with French-language skills of any level. The books contain teaching ideas and photocopiable activities which develop children's abilities to communicate in French and to appreciate French culture, customs and traditions. The activities provide opportunities for listening, speaking, reading, writing and comprehension. They will encourage children to enjoy learning the language and to feel confident about trying to speak French whenever they visit France or a French-speaking country or meet French people.

This series follows closely the Qualifications and Curriculum Authority (QCA) guidelines and scheme of work for teaching Modern Foreign Languages (MFL) in primary, middle and special schools at Key Stage 2. The books can also be used to support the teaching of French at Key Stage 3 for pupils who have had no prior teaching of the French language.

The activities in **Developing French** help children of all ages to:

- become familiar with the sounds and written form of a modern foreign language

- develop language skills and language-learning skills

- understand and communicate in a new language

- increase their cultural awareness by learning about different countries and their people

- be confident and competent in listening, reading, speaking and writing in a foreign language.

Teaching requirements

The teaching and learning activities in **Developing French** are designed to be carried out in classroom lessons or at after-school clubs. They can also be used at home. The children will benefit most if all teaching is in French, but this is by no means essential. The books can be used by a non-native speaker with at least GCE or GCSE French or secondary school French.

Pronunciation guide

When you speak French to the children, it is important that your pronunciation is as accurate as possible. A basic pronunciation guide is provided on page 8. An on-line spoken pronunciation guide linked to this book, which can be used by both teachers and pupils, is available on the A & C Black website at www.acblack.com/developingfrench

If your French needs refreshing, it's a good idea to reacquaint yourself with the language by listening to French-language tapes or CDs, watching French films or French television and using French websites. On page 62 there is a list of recommended books and websites.

Developing French Livre Un

This book covers the first units of the QCA MFL scheme of work, focusing on the following aspects of everyday life:

- greetings and introducing oneself

- counting up to 30

- being at school, classroom routine, classroom objects

- being at home, rooms of the house, furniture

- around the home and garden, pets, farmyard animals

- family, relatives and friends.

For the best results, give pupils a daily 10-minute French lesson or two 20- to 30-minute lessons each week. If this is not possible, use opportunities such as meal times, registration, games and assemblies to introduce and practise French.

Encourage the children to practise language learnt in French lessons at other times: for example, when greeting each other in corridors or when doing household jobs at home.

If you are a confident French-speaker, conduct all your lessons in French. If you are a little unsure of your French skills, using some English will make things easier and less contrived. It can also be helpful to act out situations and use mime with the children.

The book is divided into five topics. At the start of each topic are two introductory pages which provide:

- key vocabulary with translations
- grammar points
- learning objectives
- teaching ideas to introduce the topic
- notes on how to use the activity sheets
- further activities.

Key vocabulary

Each topic begins with a list of important words and phrases that are used in the activities. Where appropriate, it is indicated which words and phrases the children should learn, which are for recognition only, and which are for revision.

While faultless pronunciation is not essential, you should ensure that a clear distinction is made between such words as *un* and *une*, and *le, la* and *les*. Also be aware of instances where a mistake in pronunciation sounds like a grammatical error, such as when it is necessary to sound the final consonant of an adjective to make it into its feminine form (for example, *petit/petite*).

Teaching ideas

Also at the start of each topic there are suggestions for ways to present the new language to the pupils and to use it in a daily context or as introductions to the activity sheets.

The teaching ideas include ways of integrating French into the general school day as well as into French lessons.

Photocopiable activity sheets

These are intended to support your teaching, not to replace it. They incorporate exercises and strategies that encourage independent learning: for example, ways in which children can evaluate their own work or that of a partner.

The activities use a range of questions, puzzles, quizzes, comprehension tests and games to reinforce and extend the children's learning of French and provide opportunities for you to assess their progress. Most of the sheets are for the pupils to use individually, but some involve paired work. Some of the sheets can be used to create playing cards and flashcards for revision activities and games. These sheets will benefit from being enlarged on a photocopier before being given to the children.

The activity sheets are illustrated, where possible or relevant, with French objects, situations and scenes. We have used as the main characters a French boy and girl, Pierre and Marie. They appear throughout the book. We also introduce a number of Pierre and Marie's friends and relatives, to help children identify with French people.

Instructions and text Ensure that the children are familiar with the new vocabulary and grammar before they try out the activity sheets. All the instructions and text on the activity sheets are in French. At the start of each instruction is an icon to aid understanding. Exposing children to as much French as possible helps them to understand and communicate in the language. Translations of all headings and instructions are given at the bottom of each activity sheet.

Word banks On many of the activity sheets there is a vocabulary list (*Liste*) from which the children may choose their answers. For some activities the children will need a French–English dictionary, but it is a good idea to make one available to them at all times to reinforce vocabulary work.

Extension activities Most of the activity sheets end with a challenge (*Et maintenant* – literally 'And now'). These challenges might be appropriate for only a few children; the whole class should not be expected to complete them. Some pages provide space for the children to complete the extension activities, but for others they will need a notebook or separate sheet of paper.

Teachers' notes At the foot of each activity sheet are also teachers' notes, which include:

● translation of the instructions for the main activity and, following a bullet point (●), for the extension activity

● the learning objective

● a summary of the language skills and vocabulary children will need to practise before using the sheet

● advice on how to use the activity sheet in the classroom or at home.

These footnotes can be masked when photocopying the sheets.

Suggestions are also given for introducing the activity sheets to the children. Choose the way that you feel confident with and best suits the pupil's abilities. If possible, mime how to complete the activity sheet while reading the French instructions and pointing to the relevant parts of the sheet.

Or explain in English what the instructions mean. If you are teaching younger children or those requiring more support, you could fill in for them the first letter or word of the answers.

Differentiation Most of the activity sheets can be used in more than one way. Various possibilities are suggested, as well as ways of specifically adapting exercises to differentiate the work. Children requiring support could work in pairs.

For best results, suggest that the children fill in the sheets using a pencil rather than a pen, so that they can rub out any mistakes and not spoil the look of the finished sheet. Pupils can put their finished sheets into a folder to keep for reference.

Picture dictionaries

These illustrated spreads can be photocopied and used as revision aids. If enlarged and laminated, they can be displayed on the classroom wall. Here are some possible revision and display uses:

● make the pages the focus of a finding game: ask questions such as *Où est le chat?* or *Où sont Marie et Pierre?* The children can answer orally or point to the correct part of the picture.

● for vocabulary revision, mask or cut off the vignettes and labels around the edges and ask the children to write the French names for as many things in the illustration as they can.

● for revision of *un* or *une*, *le* or *la*, mask or cut off the border area and give each child a copy of the picture dictionary and ask them to colour in specific items that you name in French (tell them which colours to use). Or, using two different colours, they can colour-code the masculine and feminine nouns in the picture.

● for more able children, ask them to write the French names of items they can identify in the main illustration that are not shown in the dictionary around the border.

Recommended resources

On page 62 there are details of French language teaching and learning materials that you may find useful to refer to. Some will help you to brush up your language skills. Others are suitable for the pupils to investigate. Other helpful teaching resources are traditional French nursery rhymes and poems related to the topic you are teaching. Tapes and books of them are available in specialist bookshops. You will find more detailed and extensive French-language teaching plans in the QCA Modern Foreign Languages Teacher's Guide and in numerous publications from the Centre for Information on Language Teaching and Research (CILT).

Answers

You will find answers to all the questions, wordsearches and crosswords on pages 63 and 64.

Pull-out frieze

Inside the back cover of the book is a giant pull-out frieze. This can be used as the centrepiece of a permanent display in the school or classroom. The children could look in French magazines and holiday brochures for pictures to cut out and display around the frieze, such as French food, landmarks or celebrities.

Ideas for games and role-play

These work well with group or whole-class learning situations. The following ideas can be used with any topic and at any time – they can be performed as extensions to, or separate from, the activities on the photocopiable worksheets. The games can be made to last between 5 and 15 minutes, depending on the time available and how well the children respond.

Stand up/sit down game

Ask the children to stand in a circle (or at their desks if you prefer) and ask them questions in turn. If the first child gives the correct answer, he or she remains standing. If the child does not know or gives an incorrect answer, he or she should sit down in the middle of the circle (or in their seat) and you ask the same question to the next child. Continue until a correct answer is given. At this point, the children sitting down can be invited to repeat the correct answer, to include them in the rest of the game. The game can be ended at any convenient time, when one child or several children remain.

Instant reward game

This game works best if the children are sitting down on a large carpet or in the middle of the classroom. Ask questions or show visual aids for vocabulary recognition and invite volunteers to give you the correct information. Give out a reward for every correct answer (make sure the answer is completely accurate – if not, move on to another child). For rewards, use a set of reward tokens or maths interlocking cubes, or simply write points next to the children's names on your class list. Count these up at the end of the game (in French of course!). The child with the most rewards is the winner for the day/week/term.

Le pendu (Hangman)

Play this as you would play English 'Hangman' but with French words and letters called out in French. This is a good activity for learning or revising the alphabet in French.

Jacques a dit (Simon says)

Play this as you would play the game in English, but replace 'Simon says' with *Jacques a dit*. Use actions such as *levez vous* (stand up), *asseyez-vous* (sit down), *montrez la porte* (point to the door) and mimes such as *nager* (to swim), *jouer au football* (to play football), and *dessiner* (to draw).

Question/réponse

This activity lets the children practise conversation. You say the French word *Question!* and invite a child to ask a question he or she has learnt. When you say *Réponse!* any child can answer. You could write a question mark on the board and point to it every time you say *Question!* Alternatively, show a flashcard of the word.

Pronunciation guide

This page offers guidance on how to pronounce certain letters or combinations of letters in French. For each sound, an English word containing a similar sound is given. Depending on UK regional accents, use alternative sample words. Try out the sounds by reading the practice words aloud several times. It is important to use this guide in conjunction with listening to native speakers, since many of the English equivalents are approximations.

If possible, ask a French-language teacher to help you, or use the online pronunciation guide that accompanies this book on website address www.acblack.com/developingfrench

a, à	like the 'a' sound in 'rat' **practice words:** *la, chat, va, table, avion*
â	like the 'a' sound in 'car' **practice words:** *gâteau, pâtes*
e	like the 'a' sound in 'above' **practice words:** *regarde, le, cheval*
é	like the 'ay' sound in 'late' **practice words:** *écoute, réponse, légumes*
è, ê, ai	like the 'ay' sound in 'say' **practice words:** *règle, frère, être, tête, père, j'ai, chaise*
i	like the 'i' sound in 'twig' **practice words:** *lit, dix, rideau, piscine*
o	like the 'o' sound in 'pot' **practice words:** *homme, gomme,*
ô, eau, au	like the sound 'o' in 'core' **practice words:** *hôtel, beau, jaune*
u	no English equivalent but shape mouth tightly as if to say the 'aw' in 'paw' but make an 'ee' sound **practice words:** *tu, une, du, sur*
an	like the 'an' sound in 'can't' **practice words:** *dans, manger, tante, blanc*
eu	like the 'i' sound in 'sir' **practice words:** *neuf, meubles;* close mouth more for *deux, bleu*
in, ain, im	like the 'an' sound in 'sang' **practice words:** *lapin, vingt, train, pain, main, imperméable*
oi	like the 'wa' sound in 'wag' **practice words:** *trois, oiseau, poisson, toilette*
on	like the 'on' sound in 'long' **practice words:** *maison, oncle, cochon, marron*

ou	like the 'oo' sound in 'good' **practice words:** *douze, sous, mouton, boucherie*
un	like the 'an' sound in 'pant' **practice words:** *brun, lundi, un*
c	like 'k' when followed by *a, o , u* or a consonant except *h* **practice words:** *canapé, cochon, cuisine, crayon, école* like 's' when followed by *e* or *i* **practice words:** *c'est, cinq, ce*
ç	the same sound as 's' **practice words:** *ça, garçon*
ch	the same sound as 'sh' **practice words:** *douche, cochon, vache, chaise*
g	like the 'g' sound in 'good' when followed by *a, o, u, l, m* or *r* **practice words:** *gare, gomme, glace, gris, garage* like the 's' sound in 'pleasure' when followed by *e, i* or *y* **practice words:** *genou, gîte*
gn	like the 'ni' sound in 'onion' **practice words:** *araignée*
h	silent **practice words:** *histoire, hôtel, homme*
j	like the 's' sound in 'pleasure' **practice words:** *jambe, jeudi, jupe, jeu, déjeuner*
qu	like the 'c' sound in 'cat' **practice words:** *quatre, chaque, casquette, banque*
r	like a gentle dog growl **practice words:** *robe, rideau, trois, bras, rue, règle*
th	like the 't' sound in 'take' **practice words:** *thé, bibliothèque*

Topic 1: Bonjour!

Key vocabulary and grammar

To be used by the children:

Bonjour	Hello/good morning/ good afternoon
Je m'appelle…	My name is…
Et toi?	What about you?
Comment tu t'appelles?	What is your name?
Je suis un garçon/une fille	I am a boy/girl
Es-tu…?	Are you…?
Oui, Madame/Monsieur/ Mademoiselle	Yes
Ça va?	How are you?
Oui, ça va, merci	I am fine, thank you
Au revoir	Goodbye

numbers 1 to 12: *un, deux, trois, quatre, cinq, six, sept, huit, neuf, dix, onze, douze*

For recognition only:

Asseyez-vous!/Assieds-toi!	Sit down!
Levez-vous!/Lève-toi!	Stand up!/Get up!
Ecoutez!/Ecoute!	Listen!
Regardez!/Regarde!	Look!
Taisez-vous!/Tais-toi!	Be quiet!
Répétez!/Répète!	Repeat!
Très bien!	Very good!
Comptez!/Compte!	Count!
Stop!	Stop!
Je suis un homme/ une femme	I am a man/woman

Teaching ideas

Saying hello and goodbye

Once the children are sitting down at the start of the lesson, greet them with *Bonjour les enfants/la classe! Je m'appelle…* (followed by your name). Prompt them to greet you by answering *Bonjour…* (followed by your name). Do this either by saying the phrase yourself and signalling to the children to repeat it or by explaining this in English. Practise this several times.

This exchange of greetings should be used at the beginning of each lesson. Do the same for goodbye (*au revoir*) at the end of each lesson.

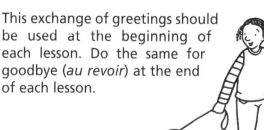

Answering the register

Call out the names on the class register and prompt each child to respond *Oui, Madame/Monsieur/ Mademoiselle!* (as appropriate). Encourage them to answer in this way every time you address a child by calling out their name.

Introducing oneself

Teach the phrase *Je m'appelle…, et toi?* by pointing to yourself on the *Je* and motioning to the child addressed on the *et toi?* Encourage the child to repeat the phrase several times.

Go round the whole group or class, with each child saying *Je m'appelle…* (followed by his or her name), *et toi?*, turning towards the next child on the *et toi?* Avoid the question coming back to you, unless you want to briefly introduce the difference between *tu* and *vous* (the polite form of address) at that point. It will be helpful to go round the group or class more than once.

Comment tu t'appelles? can be used next. Make clear the difference in response: the pupil answers with just *Je m'appelle…* (followed by his or her name), with a firm mimed 'stop!' (or the word *Stop!* itself) after the name.

You can introduce *Je suis un garçon/une fille/une femme/un homme* at various points in the above sequence by saying *Je suis une femme/un homme*, (pointing to yourself and using a picture flashcard as a visual aid), *je m'appelle…* (followed by your name). The children should respond by saying *Je suis un garçon/une fille; je m'appelle…* (followed by his or her name). Remember always to point to yourself when saying *je*.

Responding to questions

Introduce *Ça va, …?* (followed by child's name) and prompt the standard response, *Oui, ça va, merci.* When all the children have grasped this, go round the group using all three prompts in turn: *Je m'appelle…, et toi? Comment tu t'appelles?*/child's name only/*Ça va, …?* (followed by child's name). Try to catch them out and give the wrong response (they will find this amusing!).

Each of the three prompts and responses should take about 10 minutes to teach, so if combined they will fill a half-hour lesson.

You could introduce the *Question/réponse* game (see page 7) at this point. Also explain that French children put their surname first and their 'first' name second on their school work, and that their names are also called out in that way when calling the register.

Classroom routine and instructions

Start giving classroom instructions in French with hand gestures (see the illustrations in the activity on page 13). Explain the difference between *tu* (the singular, informal form of address) and *vous* (the plural or formal form of address). Once you have introduced the gestures, use them consistently from lesson to lesson. Gradually use the gestures less frequently as the spoken orders become familiar. The following list gives suggestions for hand gestures.

● *Asseyez-vous!* is indicated with both hands held palm downwards, moving up and down. For the singular form (*Assieds-toi!*) use only one hand, with the fingers pointing in the direction of the child concerned.

● *Levez-vous!* is the same gesture as *Asseyez-vous!* but with the palms facing upwards.

● For *Ecoutez!* touch both your ears. For the singular form (*Ecoute!*) touch one ear while addressing the child concerned.

● The gesture for *Regardez!* is the same as *Ecoutez!* but with your index finger pointing at your eyes.

● *Taisez-vous* or *Tais-toi* can be indicated by putting one finger on your lips.

● For *Répétez!* hold out one hand and rotate it in a circle at the wrist (showing the movement of a turning wheel).

● *Très bien!* can be shown by holding one or both thumbs up.

● To show *Comptez!* hold one hand up with the fingers splayed. With the index finger of your other hand, touch each finger tip in turn starting with the thumb.

Numbers 1 to 12

Counting up to 10 can be done with the fingers initially, but digit cards (see page 15) are an essential resource since the children must learn the numbers out of sequence, as individual words. Ensure that they do not need to count up from 1 every time.

A pair of dice is ideal for learning numbers 1 to 12. Either you or a child can throw the dice, and the children in turn say the number in French. This can be played as an instant reward game (see page 7). Alternatively, the children can say the value of each dice and then the sum of the two, for example *Deux et cinq font sept.*

Playing cards 1 to 10 can also be used for learning numbers. Try to obtain some French playing cards, since they have a 1 on the ace. As a French and numeracy activity combined, the children can say calculations and number bonds in French.

When the children write the date in their French exercise books or on the activity sheets, ask them to use the short numerical form rather than using English words (until you have taught them how to write the date in French).

Further activities

Page 11 Practising greetings The children can act out the various conversations on the activity sheet in pairs, either at their desks or in front of the class.

Page 12 Introducing oneself Reading the completed speech bubbles aloud is a good way to round off the activity and allow children working more slowly a chance to catch up.

Page 13 Understanding and giving orders Once the children are familiar with the orders, invite volunteers to play the part of the teacher in turn. They can say the phrases for the rest of the class to mime or act upon.

Page 14 Practising numbers 1 to 12 Children who complete the extension activity can add pairs of the numbers: for example, A + B, C + D, E + F. Ask them to write the calculations in words, giving them the example *Un et deux font trois.*

Page 15 Using numbers 1 to 12 This sheet can be cut into three 8-number bingo cards and used to play bingo in three teams. The teacher calls out the numbers rather than write them on the board.

For other games, cut the sheet into individual number cards. These can be sorted into numerical order or arranged in pairs to make totals of 13.

Bonjour! Ça va?

👁 **Regarde la liste.**

✏ **Choisis les mots.**

✏ **Ecris les conversations.**

Liste
Bonjour, je m'appelle Pierre, et toi?
Oui, ça va, merci.
Au revoir, Marie.
Au revoir, Pierre.
Ça va, Marie?
Je m'appelle Marie.

Invente une conversation.

Et maintenant

Translation *Hello! How are you? Look at the list. Choose the words. Write the conversations.*
• *Make up a conversation.* **Teachers' note** This activity involves practising basic greetings. The number of dashes in each speech bubble represents the number of letters in the answer. The children's own conversations can use the same phrases as the first activity, but using their name and a friend's. The children could draw themselves and a friend alongside the speech bubbles.

Developing French
Livre Un
A & C Black

11

Qui suis-je?

👁 **Regarde la liste.**

〰 **Choisis les mots.**

✏ **Complète les bulles.**

Liste
un homme
t'appelles
suis une femme
un garçon
une fille
m'appelle

Je suis
_____ .

Je m'appelle Pierre.

Je m'appelle Marie. Je suis
_____ .

Comment tu
_____ ?

Je _____
Paul.

Je suis
_____ .

Je _____
_____

Comment tu t'appelles?

Et maintenant
_____

Es-tu un garçon ou une fille?

_____

Translation *Who am I? Look at the list. Choose the words. Complete the speech bubbles.*
• *What is your name? Are you a boy or a girl?* **Teachers' note** This activity is about introducing
oneself and practising the names for people according to their age and sex (boy/girl/man/woman).
For children needing more support, use correction fluid to break up the answer lines into dashes
representing the number of letters in each word. (Do this before photocopying the sheet.)

Developing French
Livre Un
A & C Black

Les ordres

 Regarde la liste.

 Choisis les mots.

 Ecris les ordres.

Liste

Répétez!	Levez-vous!
Regardez!	Asseyez-vous!
Taisez-vous!	Ecoutez!

_____

_____

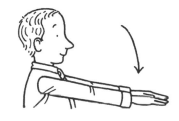

_____

_____

_____

Dessine les ordres.

Et maintenant

Très bien!   Stop!

Translation _Orders. Look at the list. Choose the words. Write the orders._ • _Draw the orders._
Teachers' note This activity helps the children to learn classroom instructions. First practise saying the orders to the children using the actions shown. Read the list aloud while pointing to the words, to help the children associate the sounds with the written words. Point out that some words are the same in French as in English – _Stop_ is used on French road signs.

Developing French
Livre Un
A & C Black

Les nombres de 1 à 12

Regarde la liste.

Complète les dominos avec les nombres.

Liste

quatre	douze
un	deux
six	11
dix	huit
4	trois
7	onze
six	onze
quatre	cinq
9	

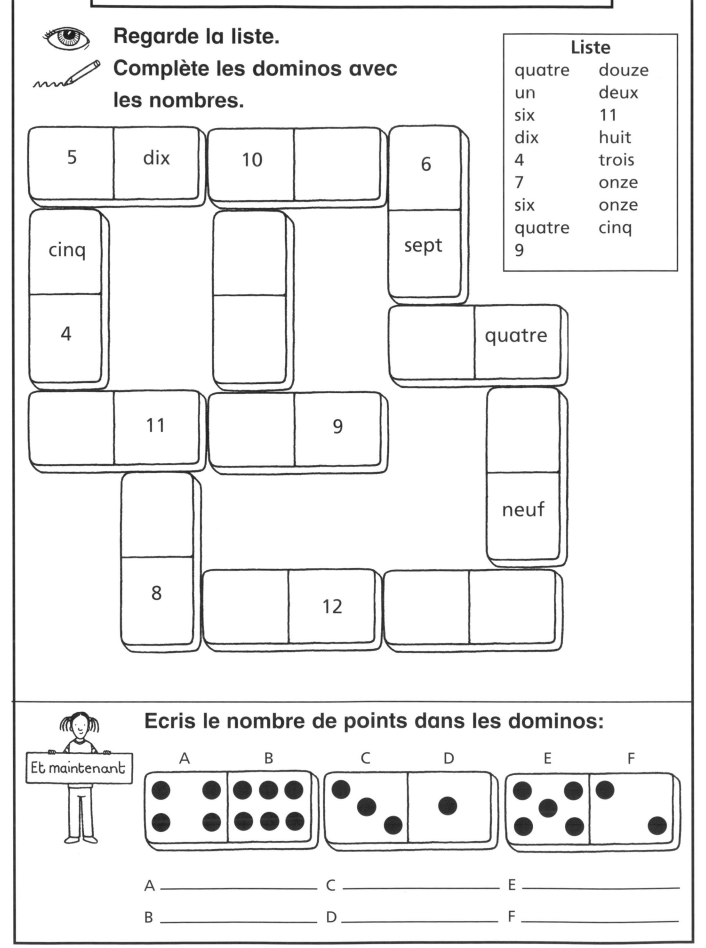

| 5 | dix |
| 10 | |
| 6 |
| cinq |
| 4 |
| sept |
| quatre |
| 11 |
| 9 |
| neuf |
| 8 |
| 12 |

Ecris le nombre de points dans les dominos:

Et maintenant

A   B   C   D   E   F

A _____   C _____   E _____

B _____   D _____   F _____

Translation *Numbers 1 to 12. Look at the list. Complete the dominoes with the numbers. • Write the number of dots on the dominoes.* **Teachers' note** First practise saying the numbers 1 to 12, both in numerical order and in random order. Hold up digit cards as prompts. Explain that the children should write the numbers in figures or words (following the sequence figure, word, figure, word, and so on around the loop). In the extension, pupils are to write the numbers in words.

Developing French
Livre Un
A & C Black

Encore des nombres

 Découpe les cartes.

 Mets les nombres en paires.

deux	11	cinq	7
3	douze	10	six
trois	5	neuf	12
4	un	8	onze
quatre	2	sept	1
6	dix	9	huit

Translation *More numbers. Cut out the cards. Put the numbers in pairs.* **Teachers' note** First practise saying numbers 1 to 12 with the class, both in numerical order and in random order. Hold up digit cards as prompts. For this activity, the children should pair up each figure card with the matching number in words. The children can use the cards to play card games such as Snap and Pelmanism. The sheet can also be used to make bingo cards (see page 10).

Developing French
Livre Un
A & C Black

Topic 2: Dans ma classe

Key vocabulary and grammar

For revision:

je suis	I am
un garçon	a boy
une fille	a girl

Vocabulary to be used by the children:

un crayon	a pencil
un stylo	a pen
un taille-crayon	a pencil sharpener
une gomme	a rubber
une règle	a ruler
une trousse	a pencil case
une table	a table
une chaise	a chair
une boîte	a box
sur	on
dans	in
devant	in front of
derrière	behind
j'ai	I have

numbers 13 to 30: *treize, quatorze, quinze, seize, dix-sept, dix-huit, dix-neuf, vingt, vingt et un, vingt-deux, vingt-trois, vingt-quatre, vingt-cinq, vingt-six, vingt-sept, vingt-huit, vingt-neuf, trente*

Grammar to be used by the children:
• masculine/feminine of 'a', 'the' and 'he/she/it':
un/une, le/la, il/elle
• plural of nouns: *les*

For recognition only:

un nombre	a number
un objet	an object
Voici…	Here is…
Qu'est-ce que c'est?	What is it?
Où est le/la…?	Where is the…?
Il/elle est…	It is…
Combien de …	
y a-t-il?	How many … are there?
Il y a…	There is/are…
Montre, montrez	Show, point to (singular and plural items)
Donne, donnez	Give (singular and plural)

Teaching ideas

Names of classroom objects

Introduce classroom words using actual classroom objects. Say the word for each object while pointing to it or holding it up for the class to see. Ask the children to repeat the word after you several times, until they have grasped the pronunciation and know which words are masculine (*un*) and which are feminine (*une*). Pupils will enjoy repeating *un, une* in quick succession several times, to give the effect of a fire engine siren! This helps them to appreciate the difference in shape of the mouth when saying the two words.

Then, hold up objects (or point to them) and ask *Qu'est-ce que c'est?* First ask the children as a group to name the objects, then encourage individual responses, giving less confident children an opportunity to repeat the answer someone else has given until they can do it independently.

It should take about 30 minutes to introduce and practise all the objects listed in the contents, and to revise *un garçon/une fille*.

Making requests

Next, pupils can be asked to take out their pencil cases and produce the various objects (or point to someone else's, if they haven't got one). Prompt the children by saying: *Montrez-moi…* (followed by the word for the object, for example *un stylo*).

Another way of reinforcing the vocabulary is to use *Donne-moi…* (followed by an object word, for example *un stylo*), *s'il te plaît. Merci.* Once the children are comfortable with the formula, they can take turns to ask each other for various items.

If the children catch on quickly you can introduce *Donnez-moi…, s'il vous plaît* (polite form), which they can use to ask you for things.

Numbers 13 to 30

Practise numbers 13 to 30 as separate words using digit cards, only counting up or down in sequence occasionally. Numbers 1 to 12 should be revised and all numbers up to 30 practised, out of sequence, for a few minutes every lesson until they are familiar.

When all numbers and classroom objects have been learnt, combine them. Hold up several objects, or a digit card next to an object, and ask *Combien de...* (followed by the plural word for the object, for example *stylos*) *y a-t-il?* or *Combien de... est-ce que tu as?* The response could be just the number, or *Il y a.../J'ai...* followed by the number and the name of the object.

Position words

Introduce positions using mime. Make one hand into a fist and use the other, held flat, to indicate the position in relation to the fist: for example, flat hand resting horizontally on top of the fist indicates *sur*; flat hand held vertically behind the fist is *derrière;* and flat hand held in front of the fist is *devant*.

When pupils understand the basic prepositions, place an object in or on something and ask *Où est le/la...?* (followed by the name of the object). The answer should be *sur/dans le/la...* (followed by the name of whatever it is positioned on or in). At first, accept *sur/dans un/une...* if the children are struggling, but progressively move on to *le/la. Il/elle est...* can be taught for recognition only or can be used by the children if they feel sufficiently confident.

Devant/derrière is best practised using people, with all the children standing one behind the other in a circle or a line. Use the question *Où est...?* (followed by a child's name). Initially the answer should be *devant/derrière* (followed by another child's name), progressing to *Je suis...* Again, *Il/elle est...* can be introduced (see above). The word *sous* for 'under' is best introduced when pupils have a wider vocabulary (see Topic 4).

Further activities

Pages 18 and 19 Matching cards and games These cards can be enlarged, glued on to card and used for quick-fire vocabulary practice. As a further extension, pupils can write new cards, one set with the French words for the objects on page 18 and another showing numbers 13 to 30 in figures. They can then use the cards to play matching pairs games, Snap and Pelmanism.

Page 18 Playing *Loto* (bingo) Divide the class into two teams. Cut the sheet in half vertically to make two *Loto* cards. Give a *Loto* card and five counters to each team. Then call out the French names of the objects on the cards, one at a time. The players in each team confer and place a counter on the correct picture if they have it. When a team covers all their objects, they should call out *Loto*. Check their card in case they have made a mistake.

Page 19 Playing *Loto* (bingo) Divide the class into three teams. Cut the sheet into thirds to make three *Loto* cards. Give a *Loto* card and six counters to each team. Play *Loto* as described above, but write the numbers on the board in figures instead of calling them out.

Pages 20 and 21 Using numbers 1 to 30 Pupils can be asked to count objects in their classroom. On page 21, as a further extension the children could be asked to write the English translation for each addition in the main activity. They could also draw their own picture like the one in the challenge and write sentences modelled on those on the sheet.

Page 22 Practising positions The children can draw and write captions for more pictures indicating positions, using the sheet as a guide. They could also write the English translations.

Page 23 Practising objects and positions In the main activity, the children could be asked to write the English translation beneath each sentence. In the challenge, children can be asked to add some more objects to the crossword (which could be fitted in reading backwards if necessary): *homme*, *crayon* and *femme*.

Page 24 Practising *J'ai* and *Je suis* The children can do additional drawings with appropriate captions on the back of the sheet. They can be asked to act out the 'speeches' in pairs or groups and make up different ones.

Page 25 Numbers game Photocopy the question mark onto card to make a game board (enlarging it if desired). The children can play in groups of four (two teams of two). They start with a counter at 1 and throw a dice in turn. They should say in French the number they have thrown. If they are correct, they move that number of spaces. They must say in French the number they land on to be allowed to stay on it. If they answer incorrectly, they must go back to their previous position. The first team to reach 30 wins. When playing games, it is a good idea to say *Bravo!* to the winners instead of using vocabulary associated with winning and losing.

Les objets dans la classe

Regarde la liste.

Choisis les mots.

Ecris les mots.

Liste

une chaise	une trousse
une fille	un crayon
une règle	un stylo
un taille-crayon	une gomme
une table	un garçon

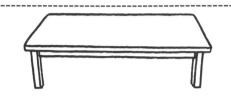

une table _____   _____

_____   _____

_____   _____

_____   _____

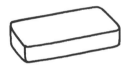

_____   _____

_____   _____

_____   _____

_____   _____

_____   _____

Et maintenant

Ecris les mots en anglais.

Dictionnaire

Translation *Objects in the classroom. Look at the list. Choose the words. Write the words.*
• *Write the words in English.* **Teachers' note** This activity involves practising names of classroom objects. To make flashcards, enlarge the sheet to A3: once the children have written the answers in French and then in English, they can glue the sheet on to card and cut along the lines. Alternatively, they can use the unlabelled pictures for card games and bingo (see page 17).

Developing French
Livre Un
A & C Black

Les nombres de 13 à 30

✂ **Découpe les cartes.**

treize	vingt	vingt-trois
dix-sept	quatorze	vingt-six
vingt et un	dix-huit	vingt-quatre
vingt-neuf	vingt-sept	quinze
vingt-huit	vingt-deux	dix-neuf
trente	seize	vingt-cinq

Translation *Numbers from 13 to 30.* *Cut out the cards.* **Teachers' note** This activity sheet is for practising the numbers 13 to 30. Ask the children to stick the sheet on to a piece of card, then cut up the sheet to make individual number cards and put them in the correct numerical order. This sheet also provides bingo cards (see page 17) which can be used on their own or with more bingo cards made with page 15.

Developing French
Livre Un
A & C Black

Combien?

 Regarde les dessins.

Regarde les mots.

 **Relie l'image et les mots.**

• quatorze taille-crayons •

• quinze gommes •

• vingt-trois crayons •

• vingt-six règles •

• treize gommes •

• trente stylos •

• vingt-sept stylos •

• seize règles •

• vingt et un crayons •

• dix-huit taille-crayons •

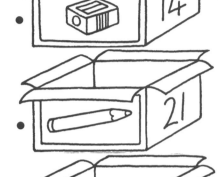

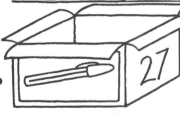

Qu'est-ce que c'est?

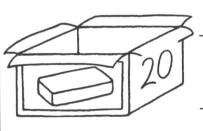

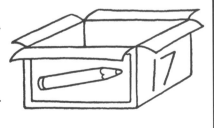

_____

_____

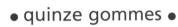

Translation *How many? Look at the pictures. Look at the words. Join the picture and the words.*
• *What is this?* **Teachers' note** This activity gives practice in the numbers 13 to 30 and the names of classroom objects. The children should be aware that each object appears twice but with different numbers.

Developing French
Livre Un
A & C Black

Addition

 Regarde les additions.

 Ecris les mots pour les chiffres.

Ecris les chiffres.

15	+	2	=	17
quinze	*et*	*deux*	*font*	*dix-sept*

quatorze	et	quatre	font	dix-huit
14	+	4	=	18

6	+	7	=	13

onze	et	cinq	font	seize

9	+	21	=	30

vingt	et	six	font	vingt-six

13	+	14	=	27

treize	et	dix-sept	font	trente

4	+	11	=	15

quatre	et	vingt et un	font	vingt-cinq

Combien d'objets y a-t-il?

 Et maintenant

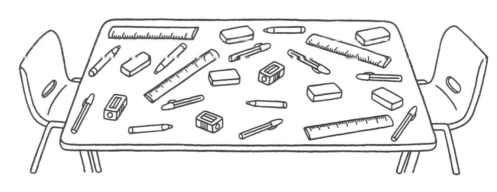

Il y a _____six_____ gommes.   Il y a _____ taille-crayons.

Il y a _____ crayons.   Il y a _____ règles.

Il y a _____ stylos.   Il y a _____ chaises.

Translation *Addition. Look at the additions. Write the words for the numbers. Write the numbers.* • *How many objects are there?* **Teachers' note** This activity gives practice in the numbers 1 to 30. To help the children, the words required for the additions all appear elsewhere on the page. If the children require more writing space, either enlarge the sheet or number the additions and ask the children to write them on another sheet of paper.

Developing French
Livre Un
A & C Black

Position

Regarde les dessins.

Regarde la liste.

Choisis les phrases.

Ecris les phrases.

Liste
Le garçon est dans la boîte.
Le garçon est derrière la fille.
La fille est devant la boîte.
Le garçon est devant la fille.
La fille est sur la boîte.
La fille est dans la boîte.

La fille est sur
la boîte.

_____
_____

_____
_____

_____
_____

_____
_____

_____
_____

Et maintenant

Regarde les mots.

Où est le garçon?

la table   la chaise

_____

_____

_____

_____

Translation *Position. Look at the drawings. Look at the list. Choose the sentences.* • *Look at the words. Where is the boy?* **Teachers' note** This activity gives practice in using words of position: *dans, sur, devant, derrière*. The children should write the correct sentence under each picture. Encourage them to check their spelling carefully.

**Developing French
Livre Un
A & C Black**

Objets et position

Regarde les phrases.

Dessine les objets.

Le crayon est sur la table.	La règle est dans la trousse.
Le garçon est devant la chaise.	La gomme est derrière le stylo.

Et maintenant

Regarde les dessins.

Ecris les mots.

1 ➤

2 ▼

3 ➤

3 ▼

5 ➤

4 ▼

7 ➤

6 ▼

8 ➤

Dictionnaire

Translation *Objects and position. Look at the sentences. Draw the objects. • Look at the drawings. Write the words.* **Teachers' note** Use this activity to reinforce learning of positions and classroom objects. The children can copy the illustrations of the objects from the picture crossword. They should use a dictionary to look up any words they are unsure of and to check their spelling.

Developing French
Livre Un
A & C Black

Qu'est-ce que j'ai?

 Regarde la liste.

 Choisis les phrases.

Ecris les phrases dans les bulles.

Liste	
Je suis un homme.	J'ai un crayon.
Je suis un homme.	J'ai une règle.
Je suis une femme.	J'ai un stylo.
Je suis une fille.	J'ai un stylo.
Je suis une fille.	J'ai un taille-crayon.
Je suis un garçon.	J'ai une trousse.

Qui es-tu?

Qu'est-ce que tu as?

Et maintenant

Translation *What have I got?* Look at the list. Choose the sentences. Write the sentences in the bubbles. • *Who are you? What have you got?* **Teachers' note** This activity combines use of the verbs *être*, to be, and *avoir*, to have. Explain that the children should choose two sentences for each person, one from each column of the list. For the extension, the children should draw themselves in the frame. They can refer to the list at the top to help them write sentences.

**Developing French
Livre Un
A & C Black**

24

Trouve les cinq objets

 Trouve les nombres.

 Ecris les lettres dans les cases.

 Trouve les cinq objets.

vingt-deux = s
treize = g
cinq = o
vingt-huit = i
deux = a
dix = y
quatre = c
six = n
quinze = m
huit = r
un = g
vingt-cinq = c
neuf = a
trente = e
onze = o
vingt-sept = a
dix-neuf = r
trois = r
vingt et un = u
douze = n
sept = c
vingt-neuf = s
vingt-quatre = e
seize = m
vingt = o
dix-sept = e
quatorze = o
vingt-trois = s
dix-huit = t
vingt-six = h

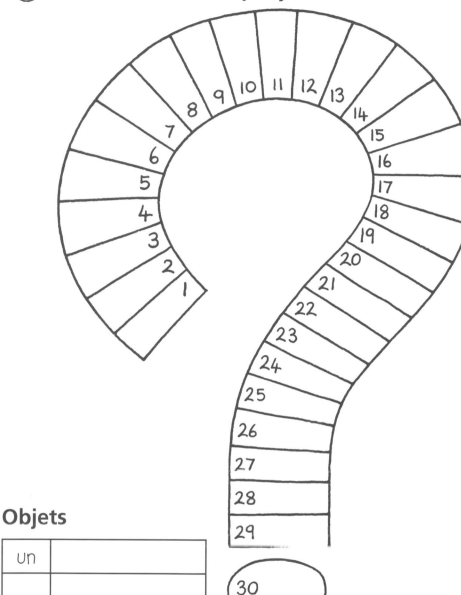

Objets

un	

 **Ecris <u>un</u> ou <u>une</u> devant les objets.**
Dessine les objets.

 Dictionnaire

---

Translation *Find the five objects. Find the numbers. Write the letters in the squares. Find the five objects.* • *Write* un *or* une *in front of the objects. Draw the objects.* **Teachers' note** This activity gives practice in using numbers 1 to 30 and the names of classroom objects. Once the children have filled in all the letters, ask them to search for the objects starting from square 1. As a further extension, you could ask them to write the English for each object.

Picture dictionary

un garçon

une fille

un crayon

une trousse

un taille-crayon

un canard
une poule
une vache
un cheval
un cochon

1 x 4 =
2 x 4 =
3 x 4 =
4 x 4 =
5 x 4 =

une gomme

une règle

un cahier d'exercices

une table

une chaise

un homme

Developing French
Livre Un
A & C Black

Dans ma classe

une
poubelle

un
professeur

derrière

devant

dans

un mot

une lettre

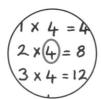

un chiffre

une
fenêtre

un
cartable

sur

Topic 3: Ma maison

Key vocabulary and grammar

For revision:

une table	a table
une chaise	a chair
dans	in
Où est...?	Where is...?

Vocabulary to be used by the children:

la maison	the house
le salon	the sitting room
la salle à manger	the dining room
la cuisine	the kitchen
la salle de bains	the bathroom
une chambre	a bedroom
le garage	the garage
un mur	a wall
une porte	a door
une fenêtre	a window
les meubles (m)	furniture
un canapé	a settee
un fauteuil	an armchair
une cuisinière	a cooker
un évier	a sink
un réfrigérateur	a refrigerator
une baignoire	a bathtub
un lavabo	a washbasin
une douche	a shower
les toilettes	the toilet
un lit	a bed
Je suis dans...	I am in...
Il/elle est dans...	He/she is in...
Ils/elles sont dans...	They are in...

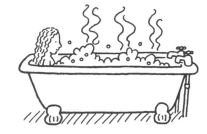

Grammar to be used by the children:

• plural of definite and indefinite articles: *un/une* become *des*; *le/la* become *les*.

For recognition only:

Va dans...!	Go into...!
Où es-tu?	Where are you?
Où est-il/elle?	Where is he/she?
Où sont-ils/elles?	Where are they?
Qu'est-ce que c'est?	What is it?

Teaching ideas

Names of rooms of the house

Introduce the vocabulary for the names of rooms and parts of the house such as walls, windows and doors. As a visual aid, show the class an enlarged version of page 31 with the room pictures cut out and glued in place on the house outline.

Where are you?

Once you have introduced the names of the rooms, play a game with the children. Lay six mats or squares of carpet on the floor to represent rooms of a house. Enlarge the pictures of the rooms on page 31. Glue each picture on to card or laminate it. Place each picture on one of the mats to show which room is which. Then ask the children, one at a time, to go into a particular room: for example *John, va dans la cuisine!* The child should go and stand on the mat representing that room. Then ask *Où es-tu?* The child replies *Je suis dans...* (followed by the name of the room they are in). To prompt the child, you can stand next to him or her and say *Je suis dans...* first. Other children in the class can then be asked *Où est-il/elle?* Encourage them to give a full answer if they can, using *Il/Elle est...*

Names of furniture and fittings

The vocabulary for furniture and fittings can be introduced next. Do this one room at a time, using enlarged versions of the pictures on page 32 as flashcards.

Once the children are familiar with this vocabulary, combine furniture and rooms with questions such as *Où est le canapé?* At first, offer a choice of two answers by asking *Dans le salon ou dans la cuisine?* As the children become more confident, they will be able to give the answer without being prompted. More advanced groups can be encouraged to reply using *Il/Elle est...*, for example *Il est dans le salon.*

Other position words such as *sur*, *devant* and *derrière* can be revised in this context. Demonstrate the positions using children and available items of furniture such as tables and chairs. You could also use pictures cut from furniture catalogues, or use dolls and dolls' house furniture.

Further activities

Page 31 Collect the rooms game Divide the class into teams of no more than four players. Photocopy the pictures of the rooms so that you have one set for each team; you keep the sets. Give each team a dice and a copy of the house outline at the bottom of the sheet. The children in the team take it in turns to roll the dice (give a signal to indicate when to roll the dice, to make sure that all the teams play at the same pace). The child who has rolled the dice should say the number in French and ask you for the room in the house represented by that number. For example, if he or she rolls a one, they should say *Le salon, s'il vous plaît*. If they ask correctly, give them their team's picture card for that room, making sure the child replies *Merci*. The first team to collect all the rooms in their house wins. To make the game last longer, you can introduce a rule that rooms have to be collected in order from 1 to 6.

Pages 31 and 32 Flashcard games These cards can be enlarged, glued on to card and used for quick-fire vocabulary practise. Hold up a card and ask *Qu'est-ce que c'est?* Alternatively, let the children make their own sets of flashcards, then ask questions which they can answer by holding up the correct card. The children could make extra sets of cards showing the French words for the rooms or objects. They can then use these with the unlabelled picture cards to play matching pairs games, Snap and Pelmanism.

Page 32 Playing *Loto* (bingo) Divide the class into two teams. Cut the sheet in half vertically to make two *Loto* cards (you could glue these on to card or laminate them). Give a *Loto* card and five counters to each team. Then call out the French names of the items of furniture on the cards, one at a time.

The players in each team confer and place a counter on the correct picture if they have it. When a team covers all their objects, they should call out *Loto*. Check their card in case they have made a mistake. The pictures of the rooms on page 31 can be photocopied to make a third bingo card (six counters will be needed).

For additional points, pupils could be asked to say the names of as many items as possible on their card.

Page 34 Giant crossword game The children could add names of rooms to the crossword, going upwards or backwards if need be: *salle à manger* or *salle de bains* can be added to cross with the 'l' of *fauteuil*; *salon* can go through the 'o' of *baignoire*; *chambre* can go upwards to the second 'r' of *réfrigérateur*; and *cuisine* can go upwards to the 'e' of *canapé*.

Page 35 Where am I? Ask the children to write what each person in the picture would say. Write a sentence on the board as an example: *Sonia – Je suis dans la salle de bains.* Alternatively, this could be done orally by nominating six children in the class to 'be' the children in the picture. Ask *Où es-tu, Sonia? Où es-tu, Thierry?* and so on, for the children to reply *Je suis dans...*

Page 37 Conjugating *être* Ask the children to draw pictures of themselves and their friends in a variety of places. They can then write sentences to describe the pictures, modelled on those on the sheet. They could also act out similar scenarios in small groups by standing/sitting in front of, behind or on furniture in the classroom. Encourage them to say a variety of phrases using different forms of the verb *être*.

Les mots dans la maison

 Regarde la liste.

 Regarde la maison.

🔍 **Trouve les mots.**

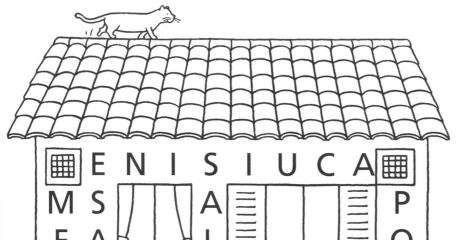
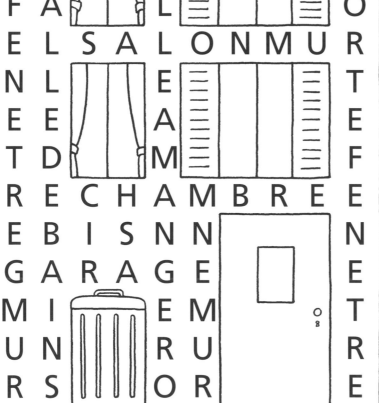

```
    E N I S I U C A
M S     A         P
F A     L         O
E L S A L O N M U R
N L     E A       T
E E     A M       E
T D     B         F
R E C H A M B R E E
E B I S N N       N
G A R A G E       E
M I     E M       T
U N     R U       R
R S     O R       E
```

Trouve le mot caché! _____

Et maintenant

☐ ☐ ☐ ☐ ☐ ☐

📖 Dictionnaire

Translation *Words in the house. Look at the list. Look at the house. Find the words.* • *Find the hidden word!* **Teachers' note** Use this activity to practise vocabulary related to the house. Point out that *mur* appears three times in the wordsearch and *fenêtre* appears twice. When the children have ringed all the listed words, they will find six unused letters. Ask them to write these in the blank boxes, then rearrange them to find the hidden word.

Developing French
Livre Un
A & C Black

Les pièces de la maison

 Découpe les pièces.

 Colle les pièces dans la maison.

Les pièces

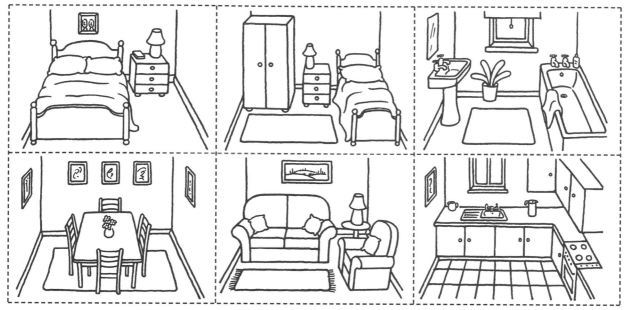

La maison

⚅ une chambre	⚄ la salle de bains	⚃ une chambre
⚀ la cuisine	⚁ la salle à manger	⚂ le salon

Translation *Rooms of the house. Cut out the rooms. Glue the rooms on to the house.*
Teachers' note This activity introduces the names for rooms of the house. The room pictures
could be enlarged and used as flashcards. This page is to be used as a game sheet (see
instructions on page 29).

Developing French
Livre Un
A & C Black

Les meubles

 Regarde la liste.

Choisis les mots.

Ecris les mots.

Liste

un canapé	un fauteuil
un lit	une cuisinière
un évier	un réfrigérateur
une baignoire	une douche
un lavabo	les toilettes

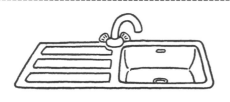 

un évier

_____   _____

_____   _____

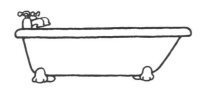 

_____   _____

 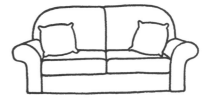

_____   _____

 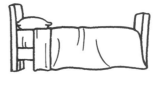

_____   _____

Translation *Furniture. Look at the list. Choose the words. Write the words.* **Teachers' note** This activity gives practice in the names of household furniture and fittings. To make flashcards, enlarge the sheet to A3: once the children have written in the answers, glue the sheet on to card and cut along the dotted lines. Alternatively, pupils can use the unlabelled pictures for card games and bingo (see page 29).

Developing French
Livre Un
A & C Black

Dans quelle pièce?

Relie les meubles et les pièces.

Dessine les meubles dans les pièces.

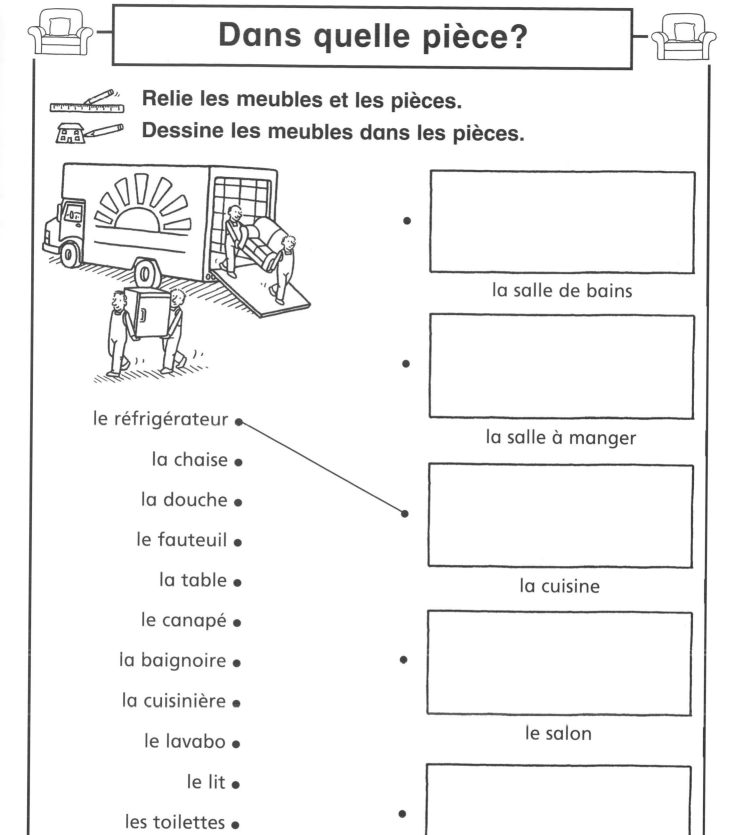

la salle de bains

la salle à manger

le réfrigérateur

la chaise

la douche

le fauteuil

la table

le canapé

la baignoire

la cuisinière

le lavabo

le lit

les toilettes

l'évier

la cuisine

le salon

une chambre

Ecris des phrases.

Exemple: Le canapé est dans le salon.

Et maintenant

Translation *In which room? Join the furniture to the rooms. Draw the furniture in the rooms.*
• *Write sentences. Example: The settee is in the sitting room.* **Teachers' note** This gives practice
in the names of rooms and furniture; using *le* and *la*; and using the verb *être*. For the extension,
the children will need a separate sheet of paper. They should write sentences stating where each
item belongs. Point out that for *les toilettes* they will need to use *sont* instead of *est*.

Developing French
Livre Un
A & C Black

Encore des meubles

   Regarde les dessins.

Regarde la liste.

 Ecris les mots.

Liste	
baignoire	fauteuil
canapé	lavabo
chaise	lit
cuisinière	réfrigérateur
douche	table
évier	toilettes

1 ►   2 ►   3 ►

6 ►   7 ►    8 ►

2

1 ▼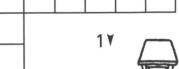

2 ▼

4 ▼

5 ▼

10 ►

9 ▼

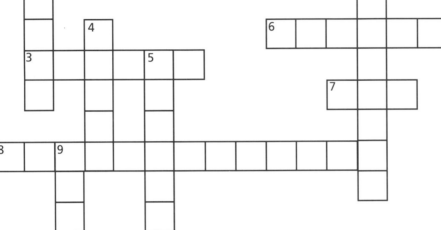

Ecris un ou une.

Et maintenant

___ baignoire   ___ douche   Dictionnaire

___ canapé   ___ évier   ___ lit

___ chaise   ___ fauteuil   ___ réfrigérateur

___ cuisinière   ___ lavabo   ___ table

Translation *More furniture. Look at the drawings. Look at the list. Write the words.* • *Write* un *or* une. **Teachers' note** Use this activity to reinforce learning the names of items of furniture. The arrows join each picture clue to the square where the first letter of the word should be written. The children may find it helpful to check the words in a dictionary before filling in the puzzle.

Developing French
Livre Un
A & C Black

Où sont-ils?

 Regarde les enfants.

 Où sont-ils?

 Regarde la liste.

 Complète les phrases.

Liste	
une chambre	le salon
la cuisine	une chambre
la salle à manger	la salle de bains

 Sonia   Pierre   Fatima   Jamel   Marie   Thierry

Sonia est ____*dans la salle de bains.*____

Pierre est ____*dans*____

Fatima est _____

Jamel est _____

Marie est _____

Thierry est _____

Et maintenant

Où est la table? _____

Où est le canapé? _____

Translation *Where are they?* Look at the children. Where are they? Look at the list. Complete the sentences. • Where is the table? Where is the settee? **Teachers' note** This gives practice in saying which room people are in. The children can draw lines linking the characters and the appropriate rooms to help them identify the characters. Once children have completed the extension, you can ask them to write similar sentences for other items of furniture.

Developing French
Livre Un
A & C Black

Où es-tu?

 Choisis la bonne réponse. ✓

Où es-tu, Sophie?

Je suis sur la table.
Je suis derrière la chaise.
Je suis derrière la table. ✓

Je suis sur la chaise.
Je suis devant la table.
Je suis dans le canapé.

Je suis devant la baignoire.
Je suis dans la baignoire.
Je suis sur la douche.

Où es-tu, Joël?

Je suis devant le réfrigérateur.
Je suis dans le lit.
Je suis sur la cuisinière.

Je suis sur le lit.
Je suis dans le fauteuil.
Je suis devant la chaise.

Je suis dans la cuisinière.
Je suis sur les toilettes.
Je suis derrière la cuisinière.

Et maintenant

Dessine où tu es.

Ecris où es-tu.

Je suis _____

Translation *Where are you?* Choose the correct answer. • *Draw where you are. Write where you are.* **Teachers' note** This gives practice in saying where you are; names of items of furniture; and using *Je suis*. The children should tick the correct answer from the three choices under each picture. For the extension, they should describe where they are in relation to furniture in the classroom.

Developing French
Livre Un
A & C Black

Être

Regarde la liste.

Complète les phrases.

Liste

suis	est	sont
es	sommes	sont
est	êtes	

Je _____ dans le jardin.

Nous _____ dans le jardin.

Tu _____ dans le garage.

Ils _____ dans la maison.

Vous _____ dans la maison.

Il _____ sur le mur.

Elle _____ derrière le mur.

Elles _____ derrière le mur.

Ecris les phrases.

Et maintenant

_____

_____

_____

_____

Translation To be. *Look at the list. Complete the sentences.* • *Write the sentences.*
Teachers' note This activity gives practice in conjugating the verb *être*. Remind the children of the masculine and feminine, singular and plural forms. Point out that *est* and *sont* appear in the list twice and so should be used twice in the answers. For the extension activity, the children can use the grammar and vocabulary on the rest of the page to help them write the sentences.

Developing French
Livre Un
A & C Black

37

Picture dictionary

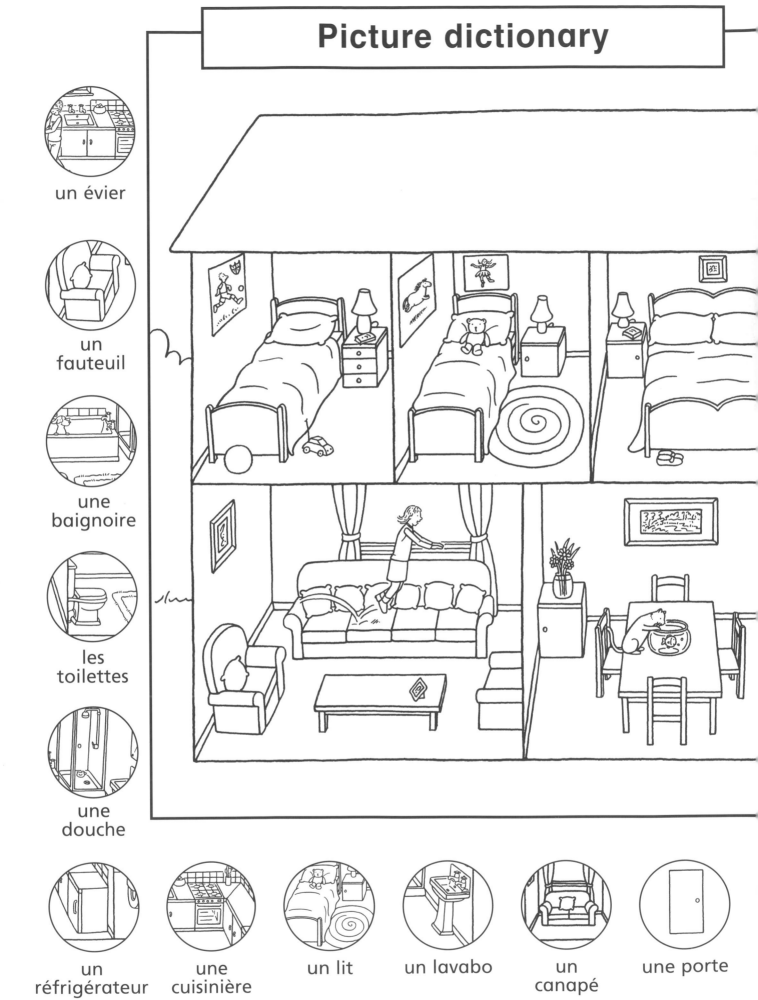

un évier

un fauteuil

une baignoire

les toilettes

une douche

un réfrigérateur

une cuisinière

un lit

un lavabo

un canapé

une porte

Developing French: Livre Un
A & C Black

Ma maison

un garçon

une fille

un chien

un poisson

un chat

un mur

une fenêtre

le garage

une table

une chaise

une glace

Developing French
Livre Un
A & C Black

Topic 4: Les animaux

Key vocabulary and grammar

For revision:

sur	on
dans	in
devant	in front of
derrière	behind

Vocabulary to be used by the children:

un animal	an animal
un chat	a cat
un chien	a dog
un mouton	a sheep
un cochon	a pig
un canard	a duck
un oiseau	a bird
un cheval	a horse
une vache	a cow
une poule	a hen
une souris	a mouse
un poisson	a fish
un lapin	a rabbit
un hamster	a hamster
une araignée	a spider
J'aime…	I like…
Je n'aime pas…	I don't like…
sous	under

Grammar to be used by the children:

• irregular plurals: *animal/animaux; cheval/ chevaux; oiseau/oiseaux; souris/souris*

For recognition only:

J'ai un(e)…	I have a…
Je n'ai pas de….	I don't have a…
Qu'est-ce que c'est?	What is it?
miaou	miaow
ouah, ouah	woof, woof
bêêêê	baa
coin, coin	quack, quack
cui, cui	tweet, tweet
hiiiiiii	neigh
meuh	moo
cot, cot, codète	cluck, cluck

Teaching ideas

Animal flashcards
Make flashcards of the first ten animals in the list by enlarging page 42 and cutting out the pictures. Hold up a picture and ask the children *Qu'est-ce que c'est?* You could also prompt the children with the sound the animal makes in French (see page 43). Soft toys could be used instead of flashcards.

Alternatively, show the children a picture, for example one of a duck, and ask *C'est un chat? C'est un cochon? C'est une vache?* and so on. The children should respond *Non* each time until you say *C'est un canard?* The response should then be *Oui* or *Oui, c'est un canard*.

When the children know these ten animals, others can be added progressively using picture flashcards or toy animals. The pictures on page 45 could also be enlarged to make flashcards.

Questions about pets
Practise *J'ai un/une…* (followed by the name of an animal) by giving out flashcards or toy animals to the children and inviting them to say which animal they have. Progress to asking them about their pets at home. This can be done either in English or in French using the question *Tu as des animaux à la maison?* The children should reply *Oui, j'ai un/une…* (followed by the name of the animal) or *Non* (followed by *Je n'ai pas d'animaux à la maison* as an optional extra).

Likes and dislikes
J'aime… and *Je n'aime pas…* can be introduced using smiling and grimacing faces as on page 44. You could make your own flashcards of faces or use mime. Hold up a picture of an animal or a toy and ask the children one at a time *Tu aimes les chiens/les chats/les souris…?* Accept short answers, (*Oui* or *Non*), but encourage the children to give a full answer using *J'aime…* or *Je n'aime pas…* if possible.

Plurals of nouns
Page 44 can be used to introduce the concept of regular and irregular plurals. For regular plurals, simply add an *s*. If the word already ends in *s* in the singular, there is no change for the plural. Most words ending in *u* take an *x* instead of an *s* (exceptions to this rule can be explained much later). Many words ending in *al* change to *aux* in the plural. These irregular plurals can be learnt individually as the children come across them.

Combining topics

To combine the topic of animals with numbers, hold up number cards and pictures of animals to revise saying how many you have of something. To combine with rooms of the house, make a large plan of a house using the pictures of rooms on page 31. (To do this, lay six mats or squares of carpet on the floor to represent rooms of a house. Enlarge the pictures of the rooms and place each picture on one of the mats to show which room is which.) Place animal flashcards or toy animals in the rooms. Then ask the children where the animals are: *Où est le chat/le chien/la vache…?* The children should answer *Dans le salon/la cuisine/une chambre…* or *Il/Elle est dans le salon/la cuisine/une chambre…* To combine the topic with revision of furniture and position, place toy animals on, in, in front of or behind items of doll's furniture. Ask the children where the animals are, as above.

Further activities

Page 42 Practising names of animals These cards can be enlarged, glued on to card and used for quick-fire vocabulary practise. Hold up a card and ask *Qu'est-ce que c'est?* Alternatively, let the children make their own sets of flashcards, then ask questions which they can answer by holding up the correct card. The children could make extra sets of cards showing the French words for the animals. They can then use these with the unlabelled picture cards to play matching pairs games, Snap and Pelmanism.

Page 42 Playing *Loto* (bingo) Divide the class into two teams. Cut the sheet in half vertically to make two *Loto* cards (you could glue these on to card or laminate them). Give a *Loto* card and five counters to each team. Play *Loto* according to the instructions on page 17.

Page 42 Guessing game Guessing games are always popular with children. Play this game with the whole class. Pick a card without showing the children and and invite them to guess what animal it is by asking *C'est un chien? C'est un oiseau? C'est une poule?* and so on. The teacher responds either *Non* or *Oui, c'est un…* (followed by the name of the animal). The child who guesses correctly, without making a mistake in the French, may then pick a card for the others to guess.

Page 43 Animal sounds The children could make a set of eight cards showing the French animal sounds. They can then combine these with the eight corresponding picture cards from page 42. These can be used to play matching pairs games, Snap and Pelmanism, to reinforce the names of animals and the sounds they make.

Page 44 Plurals of animal nouns The children can refer to this sheet to help them learn the singular and plural forms of each animal name. Ask them to draw a chart with two columns. In the first column they write the singular, for example *le chat, le chien*. In the second column they write the plural, for example *les chats, les chiens*. Encourage them to illustrate their charts.

Page 45 Finding out more animal names This activity offers an opportunity for the children to find out the French names of other animals. Encourage them to use a dictionary to look up any animals they wish, including zoo animals. They should draw each animal and label it. The whole class could contribute to a 'zoo' wall frieze showing a variety of labelled animals. They could write sentences about the animals like those on the activity sheet, for example *Je n'ai pas de lion*.

Page 46 Where are the animals? Once the children have completed the activity, they can draw more animals in the picture and write sentences describing where they are. The picture could also be enlarged to use as a visual aid for whole-class oral work. Play guessing games: cover each room of the house with a separate piece of paper, attached with sticky putty. Ask a question such as *Où est le lapin?* Invite the children to guess by saying for example *Il est dans le salon?* Uncover the rooms as the children guess, to show whether their guess is correct or incorrect. Encourage the child who guesses correctly to say the answer in a full sentence, for example *Le lapin est dans la salle à manger*.

Page 47 Animal names The children could add the names of other animals to the crossword, writing them backwards and/or upwards if need be. They could also make a crossword or wordsearch of their own and give it to a friend to solve.

Les animaux

 Regarde la liste.

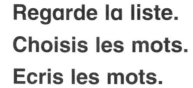 **Choisis les mots.**

Ecris les mots.

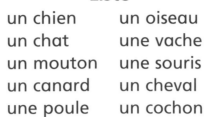

Liste

un chien	un oiseau
un chat	une vache
un mouton	une souris
un canard	un cheval
une poule	un cochon

 **Dictionnaire**

un chien

_____

_____

_____

_____

_____

_____

_____

_____

_____

_____

Translation *Animals. Look at the list. Choose the words. Write the words.* **Teachers' note** This activity introduces the names of some common animals. To make flashcards, enlarge the sheet to A3: once the children have written in the answers, they can glue the sheet on to card and cut along the dotted lines. Alternatively, they can use the unlabelled pictures for card games and bingo (see page 41).

42

Developing French
Livre Un
A & C Black

Quel animal?

 Regarde les dessins.

 Réponds aux questions.

le chat

Quel animal fait 'miaou'?

le chat

Quel animal fait 'coin, coin'?

_____

Quel animal fait 'ouah, ouah'?

_____

Quel animal fait 'cui, cui'?

_____

Quel animal fait 'bêêêê'?

_____

Quel animal fait 'meuh'?

_____

Quel animal fait 'cot, cot, codète'?

_____

Quel animal fait 'hiiiiiii'?

_____

la vache

l'oiseau

la poule

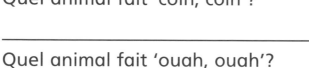

le cheval

le canard

le chien

le mouton

Ecris l'anglais.

Et maintenant

miao _miaow_ _____

coin, coin _____

ouah, ouah _____

cui, cui _____

bêêêê _____

meuh _____

cot, cot, codète _____

hiiiiiii _____

Translation *Which animal? Look at the drawings. Answer the questions.* • *Write the English.*
Teachers' note In this activity, the children practise the names of animals and find out how the French represent the sound each animal makes. Encourage the children to say the animal sounds aloud in French and in English – they will discover how even animals in France speak a different language!

**Developing French
Livre Un
A & C Black**

Tu aimes les animaux?

 Regarde les deux possibilités.

Choisis les mots.

Ecris ton opinion.

J'aime...   Je n'aime pas...

_____ les chats.

_____ les chiens.

_____ les moutons.

_____ les vaches.

_____ les canards.

_____ les poules.

_____ les cochons.

_____ les souris.

_____ les oiseaux.

_____ les chevaux.

_____ les animaux.

Ecris l'opinion de ton partenaire.

Et maintenant _____

_____

_____

_____

Liste
Il aime
Elle aime
Il n'aime pas
Elle n'aime pas

Translation *Do you like animals? Look at the two possibilities. Choose the words. Write your opinion.* • *Write your partner's opinion.* **Teachers' note** This activity introduces the plural form of the names of animals. The children could draw lines joining each sentence to the matching animal illustration, to show their understanding of the vocabulary. For the extension, the children will need to work in pairs. They could ask each other questions, for example *Tu aimes les chats?*

Developing French
Livre Un
A & C Black

Tu as des animaux?

 Regarde les questions.

 Choisis les bonnes réponses. ✓

 Tu as un chat?

Oui, j'ai un chat.
Non, je n'ai pas de chat.

 Tu as un oiseau?

Oui, j'ai un oiseau.
Non, je n'ai pas d'oiseau.

 Tu as une araignée?

Oui, j'ai une araignée.
Non, je n'ai pas d'araignée.

 Complète les phrases.

 Tu as un chien?

Oui, j'ai _____ chien.
Non, je n'ai pas _____.

 Tu as un hamster?

Oui, j'ai _____.
Non, _____ de hamster.

 Tu as un cheval?

_____ , j'ai un cheval.
Non, je n'ai pas _____.

 Tu as un lapin?

Oui, j'ai _____.
Non, _____ de lapin.

 Tu as un poisson?

Oui, _____.
Non, _____.

 **Dessine un autre animal.**
Comment s'appelle-t-il en français?

Dictionnaire

Translation *Do you have any animals? Look at the questions. Choose the correct answers.*
Complete the sentences. • Draw another animal. What is it called in French? **Teachers' note** In
this activity the children revise the names of animals and say which pets they do and do not have.
Help them to find the French names of other animals using a dictionary. Children who have pets
can draw them and write their names, for example *Mon chat s'appelle Trevor.*

**Developing French
Livre Un
A & C Black**

Où sont-ils?

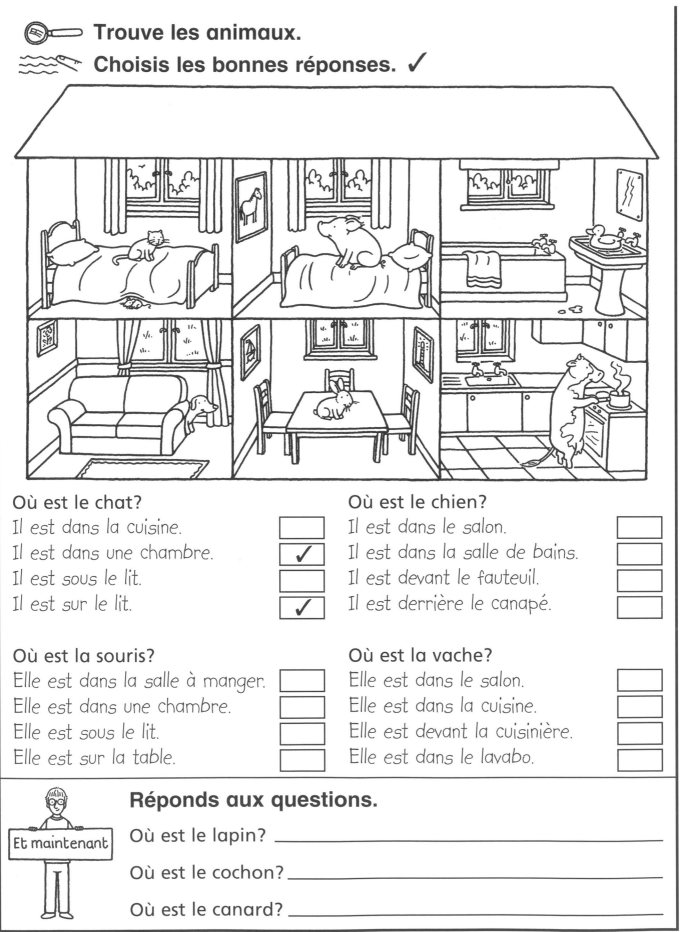

Trouve les animaux.

Choisis les bonnes réponses. ✓

Où est le chat?

Il est dans la cuisine. ☐

Il est dans une chambre. ✓

Il est sous le lit. ☐

Il est sur le lit. ✓

Où est le chien?

Il est dans le salon. ☐

Il est dans la salle de bains. ☐

Il est devant le fauteuil. ☐

Il est derrière le canapé. ☐

Où est la souris?

Elle est dans la salle à manger. ☐

Elle est dans une chambre. ☐

Elle est sous le lit. ☐

Elle est sur la table. ☐

Où est la vache?

Elle est dans le salon. ☐

Elle est dans la cuisine. ☐

Elle est devant la cuisinière. ☐

Elle est dans le lavabo. ☐

Réponds aux questions.

Et maintenant

Où est le lapin? _____

Où est le cochon? _____

Où est le canard? _____

Translation *Where are they? Find the animals. Choose the correct answers.* • *Answer the questions.* **Teachers' note** This activity combines practising the nouns for animals, questions using *Où est…?* and positions of objects. Point out to the children that they should tick two answers for each question. For the extension activity, the answers can be found among the choices provided for the main activity.

Developing French
Livre Un
A & C Black

Trouve les animaux

👁 **Regarde la liste.**

👁 **Regarde les dessins.**

✎ **Ecris les mots.**

Liste

chat	poule
chien	oiseau
cochon	lapin
canard	mouton
vache	cheval
poisson	souris

1 ►   7 ►   9 ►

3 ►   5   10 ►   11 ►

	2		3	4									
1							6		7	8			
	9					10							
										11			

8▼

2▼   3▼   4▼   5▼   6▼

👧 **Et maintenant**

Ecris un ou une devant les mots.

Dictionnaire

_____ chat   _____ vache   _____ lapin

_____ chien   _____ poisson _____ mouton

_____ cochon _____ poule   _____ cheval

_____ canard _____ oiseau   _____ souris

Translation *Find the animals. Look at the list. Look at the drawings. Write the words.* • *Write un or une in front of the words.* **Teachers' note** This involves practising the names and genders of animals. The children can use a dictionary to help them identify the animals and complete the crossword. Emphasise the importance of using the correct gender for nouns.

Developing French
Livre Un
A & C Black

47

Picture dictionary

un chat

un chien

un mouton

un cochon

un canard

un oiseau

un cheval

une vache

une poule

une souris

un poisson

48

Developing French
Livre Un
A & C Black

Les animaux

un tracteur

une fenêtre

une porte

une fleur

un arbre

un lapin

une araignée

une grenouille

un cygne

un fermier

une ferme

Developing French
Livre Un
A & C Black

49

Topic 5: Ma famille

Key vocabulary and grammar

For revision:

j'ai	I have
un homme	a man
une femme	a woman
un garçon	a boy
une fille	a girl

Vocabulary to be used by the children:

la famille	the family
le père	the father
la mère	the mother
le grand-père	the grandfather
la grand-mère	the grandmother
le fils	the son
la fille	the daughter
le frère	the brother
la sœur	the sister
l'oncle	the uncle
la tante	the aunt
le cousin	the cousin (male)
la cousine	the cousin (female)
Il s'appelle…	He is called…
Elle s'appelle…	She is called…
Je voudrais…	I would like…
le père de (Marie)	(Marie)'s father
la mère de (Marie)	(Marie)'s mother
mon père	my father
ma mère	my mother
ton père	your father
ta mère	your mother
son père	his/her father
sa mère	his/her mother
Je suis fils unique/	
Je suis fille unique	I am an only child

For recognition only:

Qui est-ce?	Who is it?
Qu'est-ce que c'est?	What is it?
moi	me

Teaching ideas

Nouns for family members

Revise *un homme, une femme, un garçon* and *une fille* by drawing one of each on the board and labelling them (matchstick people will be fine). Alternatively, use flashcards or an enlarged copy of the characters on page 12.

Then draw a family on the board consisting of a man, a woman, a girl and a boy. It can be helpful to draw the parents holding hands with the children to reinforce the relationship between them. Point to the man and say *C'est le père*. Point to the woman and say *C'est la mère*. Point to the girl and say *C'est la fille*. Finally, point to the boy and say *C'est le fils*. Ask the children to repeat the sentences after you a few times. Make sure they are confident with the irregular pronunciation of *fils* (the *s* is pronounced but the *l* is not). Then ask *Qui est-ce?* or *Qu'est-ce que c'est?* as you point to one of the people. The children should reply *C'est le père/la mère/le fils/la fille*.

When the children are confident with this, draw two more people to represent grandparents (if you are drawing matchstick people, you could draw them with a walking stick). Point to the new characters in turn and say *C'est le grand-père. C'est la grand-mère*.

Then teach the children to recognise *le père de…/la mère de…* and so on. Make up names for all the people in the drawing and write them on the board. Then ask *Qui est le père de…?* (followed by the name of the son or daughter), *Qui est le fils de…?* (followed by the name of the mother or father) and so on for each member of the family.

Introducing family members

To teach *mon/ma* you could draw your own family, with your parents and children (if you have any). Label the people with their names, and write *moi* under the person representing you in the picture. Ask the question *Comment s'appelle mon père?* and answer it yourself by saying *Mon père s'appelle…* Repeat for the other members of your family, reinforcing the use of *mon* and *ma*.

Then ask the children, one at a time, *Comment s'appelle ton père?* They should begin their answer *Mon père s'appelle…* Go round the class again asking *Comment s'appelle ta mère?* This can also be done for *le grand-père* and *la grand-mère*. Remember to be sensitive to any children in the class who have one-parent families or who are separated from their families.

When the children are confident, introduce *le frère* and *la sœur* and use the same exercise to practise *Mon frère/ma sœur s'appelle...* Children who have no brothers or sisters can be encouraged to use the phrase *Je suis fils unique/Je suis fille unique*. After this you can add aunts, uncles and cousins. Explain to the children that in French there are two words for 'cousin' and ensure they use the correct one. If any children in the class have stepbrothers and stepsisters, encourage them to talk about them using *Mon demi-frère/ma demi-sœur s'appelle...*

Family photographs

You could bring in family group photographs to use as visual aids. The children can also be invited to bring their own family photographs to school. Let  them show their photographs to the whole class, saying who the people are and what they are called. The family trees on pages 52 and 53 can also be used as class visual aids (enlarge them on a photocopier).

Further activities

Page 52 Family photos These pictures can be enlarged, together or separately, to be used as class visual aids. Using the pictures separately, ask *Qui est-ce?* as you hold up one of the people. The children should reply *C'est le grand-père/la grand-mère/le père/la mère/le fils/la fille*. Using all the pictures as they are arranged on the page, ask questions such as *Qui est le père de Benjamin? Qui est la sœur de Benjamin?* The children reply *C'est Etienne/C'est Claire*.

Page 53 Family tree This family tree can be enlarged to use as a class visual aid to teach, reinforce or test the family vocabulary. Ask questions such as *Qui est le frère de Sonia? Qui est la mère de Sonia?* The children reply *C'est Paul/C'est Geneviève*.

Page 54 Family relations This sheet can be used for recording how many brothers and sisters each child in the class has. Enlarge and cut out the sentences in the centre of the page. Organise a class survey, where you ask the pupils in turn to write their names next to the appropriate sentences. Help the children to write new sentences if they need to.

Pages 56–57 Happy Families To play Happy Families, divide the class into four teams. Give out three cards to each team. Put the remaining cards on your desk. In turn, a child from each team asks another team of their choice: *Dans la famille... (Chat/Chien/Cochon/Mouton) je voudrais...* (followed by one of the family members, such as *le grand-père*). They must already have at least one member of that family in order to be able to ask for another. If the team they ask has the card, they must hand it over. Otherwise, the team doing the asking picks up from the pile. The team who was asked then has the next turn. The first team to make a complete family is the winner. When playing games, it is a good idea to say *Bravo!* to the winners instead of using vocabulary associated with winning and losing.

These pictures can also be enlarged to use as visual aids. Using two sets of the cards, groups of children can play other games such as matching pairs, Snap and Pelmanism.

Page 56–57 Guessing game Play this guessing game with the whole class. Pick a card without showing the children and invite them to guess who it is by asking *C'est le grand-père/la grand-mère/le père/la mère/le fils/la fille?* The teacher responds either *Non* or *Oui, c'est le/la...* The child who guesses correctly, without making a mistake in the French, may then pick a card for the others to guess.

Page 58 Story Ask the children to look for particular things in the story and underline them using different coloured pencils, for example, rooms of the house, words for family members and number words. The children could also choose parts of the story to illustrate for a display.

Photos de famille

Regarde les phrases.

Ecris les noms sous les photos.

_____   _____

_____   Benjamin   _____

Je m'appelle Benjamin.

- Mon frère s'appelle Thomas.
- Ma sœur s'appelle Claire.
- Mon père s'appelle Etienne.

- Ma mère s'appelle Emilie.
- Mon grand-père s'appelle Yves.
- Ma grand-mère s'appelle Juliette.

Dessine trois membres de ta famille.

Qui est-ce?

Et maintenant

_____

Translation *Family photos. Look at the sentences. Write the names under the photos.* • *Draw three members of your family. Who are they?* **Teachers' note** Use this activity to practise ways of introducing members of the family. Explain to the children how a family tree is arranged. For the extension activity, encourage the children to label their drawings saying what relation each person is to themselves, for example *ma mère, mon frère*.

Developing French
Livre Un
A & C Black

La famille de Sonia

 Regarde la famille de Sonia.

 Regarde la liste.

Complète les phrases.

Liste	
le grand-père	le frère
la grand-mère	la sœur
le père	le fils
la mère	la fille

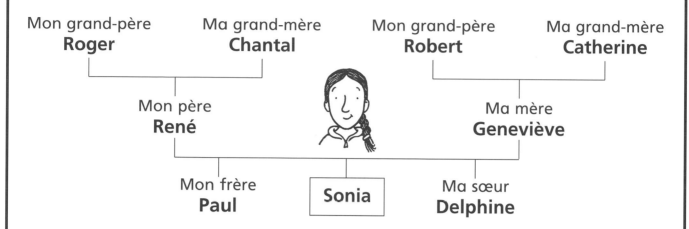

Mon grand-père **Roger** Ma grand-mère **Chantal** Mon grand-père **Robert** Ma grand-mère **Catherine**

Mon père **René** Ma mère **Geneviève**

Mon frère **Paul** **Sonia** Ma sœur **Delphine**

l'arbre généalogique

Roger est _____ de Sonia.   Sonia est _____ de René.

René est _____ de Sonia.   Paul est _____ de René.

Catherine est _____ de Sonia.

Geneviève est_____ de Sonia.

Paul est _____ de Sonia.

Delphine est_____ de Sonia.

Regarde la famille de Sonia.

Ecris encore des phrases.

_____

_____

_____

Translation *Sonia's family. Look at Sonia's family. Look at the list. Complete the sentences.*
• *Look at Sonia's family. Write more sentences.* **Teachers' note** This activity helps to reinforce the
names for family members. Once the children have completed the activity sheet, they could try
writing similar sentences using the names of people in their family.

Developing French
Livre Un
A & C Black

Qui est-ce?

 Regarde les dessins.

 Regarde les phrases.

Qui est-ce?

Alice

Marie

Je suis fils unique.

C'est Fabien.

J'ai un frère et une sœur.

_____

J'ai trois sœurs.

Fabien

Marc

_____

Je suis fille unique.

_____

J'ai deux frères.

_____

J'ai deux frères et une sœur.

Karim

David

_____

J'ai trois frères.

_____

J'ai deux sœurs.

_____

Sophie

Julie

 **Combien de frères et sœurs as-tu?**

_____

_____

Translation *Who is it? Look at the drawings. Look at the sentences. Who is it?* • *How many brothers and sisters do you have?* **Teachers' note** This activity involves understanding and using phrases about members of the family. Encourage the children to ask each other how many brothers and/or sisters they have.

Developing French
Livre Un
A & C Black

Trouve la famille

 Regarde la liste.

 Trouve les mots.

G	R	A	N	D	M	E	R	E
R	M	S	F	R	E	R	E	C
A	S	L	I	F	R	E	M	O
N	F	I	L	L	E	P	E	U
D	R	F	S	O	E	U	R	S
P	E	R	E	T	N	E	E	I
E	R	I	N	L	F	C	A	N
R	E	A	L	F	I	L	L	E
E	T	C	O	U	S	I	N	E

Liste

grand-père
grand-mère
père
père
mère
mère
fils
fils
fils
fille
fille
oncle
tante
frère
frère
soeur
cousin
cousine

Trouve le mot caché!

Et maintenant

☐ ☐ ☐ ☐ ☐ ☐ ☐

Translation *Find the family. Look at the list. Find the words.* • *Find the hidden word!*
Teachers' note This activity helps to reinforce the names of family members. Point out that some of the words appear twice, as indicated in the list. Explain that the words run straight across, down and diagonally. When the children have ringed all the words, they will find seven unused letters. Ask them to write these in the blank boxes, then rearrange them to find the hidden word.

Developing French
Livre Un
A & C Black

Les quatre familles: 1

✂ **Découpe les cartes.**

Famille Chat  Le grand-père	**Famille Chat**  La grand-mère	**Famille Chat**  Le père
Famille Chat  La mère	**Famille Chat**  Le fils	**Famille Chat**  La fille
Famille Chien  Le grand-père	**Famille Chien**  La grand-mère	**Famille Chien**  Le père
Famille Chien  La mère	**Famille Chien**  Le fils	**Famille Chien**  La fille

Translation *Four families: 1. Cut out the cards.* **Teachers' note** Use the cards to play Happy Families. See page 51 for an explanation of how to play.

Developing French
Livre Un
A & C Black

Les quatre familles: 2

✂ **Découpe les cartes.**

Famille Cochon  Le grand-père	**Famille Cochon**  La grand-mère	**Famille Cochon**  Le père
Famille Cochon  La mère	**Famille Cochon**  Le fils	**Famille Cochon**  La fille
Famille Mouton  Le grand-père	**Famille Mouton**  La grand-mère	**Famille Mouton**  Le père
Famille Mouton  La mère	**Famille Mouton**  Le fils	**Famille Mouton**  La fille

Translation *Four families: 2. Cut out the cards.* **Teachers' note** Use the cards to play Happy Families. See page 51 for an explanation of how to play.

Developing French
Livre Un
A & C Black

57

Une histoire

Boucle d'or et les trois ours

Il était une fois une petite fille qui s'appelait Boucle d'or.
Elle habitait dans une petite maison près d'une forêt.
Dans la forêt habitaient trois ours: Papa ours, Maman
ours et Bébé ours.

Un jour, Boucle d'or est entrée dans la forêt. Elle a vu la maison des trois
ours. Elle est entrée dans la cuisine. Elle a vu trois bols de soupe sur la
table – un très grand bol, un bol moyen et un petit bol. Alors, avec une
cuillère, Boucle d'or a goûté la soupe du grand bol. Mais la soupe était
trop chaude. Puis Boucle d'or a goûté la soupe du bol moyen, mais elle
était trop froide. Alors elle a goûté celle du petit bol et comme elle était
juste bien, elle a tout mangé!

Puis Boucle d'or a vu quatre chaises – deux grandes chaises, une chaise
moyenne et une petite chaise. D'abord elle a essayé de monter sur une
grande chaise, mais elle était trop haute. Ensuite elle a essayé la chaise
moyenne, mais elle s'est cassée. Alors elle a essayé la petite chaise et elle
était juste bien. Elle est restée assise un petit peu pour se reposer.

Ensuite Boucle d'or est montée dans la chambre où elle a vu trois lits –
un grand lit, un lit moyen et un petit lit. Elle a essayé de monter dans le
grand lit, mais il était trop haut. Puis elle est montée dans le lit moyen,
mais il n'était pas confortable. Alors elle est montée dans le petit lit et
comme il était juste bien, elle s'est endormie.

Un peu plus tard, les trois ours sont rentrés à la maison. Quand ils sont
entrés dans la cuisine, Papa ours a dit: 'Qui a touché à ma soupe?' et
Maman ours a dit: 'Qui a touché à ma soupe?' et Bébé ours a dit: 'Qui a
mangé toute ma soupe?' (snif, snif).

Puis Papa ours a dit: 'Qui a touché à ma chaise?' et Bébé ours a dit: 'Qui
a touché à ma chaise?' et Maman ours a dit: 'Qui a touché à ma chaise
et l'a cassée?' (grr, grrr).

Puis les trois ours sont montés dans la chambre. Papa ours a dit: 'Qui a
touché à mon lit?' et Maman ours a dit: 'Qui a touché à mon lit?' et
Bébé ours a dit: 'Qui a touché à mon lit et est encore dedans?!'

Alors Boucle d'or s'est réveillée en sursaut. En voyant les trois ours elle
s'est sauvée en courant. Elle a couru jusqu'à sa maison sans s'arrêter!

Teachers' notes Use this with page 59. Tell the pupils that the story is *Goldilocks and the Three Bears* – but with a few changes – so they can work out the storyline even though they may not understand every word in French. Give the children copies of the story and read it aloud, encouraging them to follow the text as you do so. Then give them page 59 for them to answer the comprehension questions.

Developing French
Livre Un
A & C Black

Compréhension

Answer these questions about the story of <u>Boucle d'or et les trois ours.</u> Write your answers in English.

Dictionnaire

1. Where did the three bears live? _____

2. What was in the bowls? _____

3. How many chairs were there? _____ What sizes were they?

_____

4. Whose chair did Goldilocks break? _____

5. Which bed did Goldilocks find uncomfortable? _____

6. Which was the first bear to speak? _____

7. What did Daddy Bear say when he went into the bedroom?

_____

8. What did Goldilocks do when she saw the bears?

_____

Et maintenant

Find words for household objects in the story.
List them in French and in English.
Example: *un bol   a bowl*

Teachers' notes Use this with page 58. The questions relate to the story of *Goldilocks and the Three Bears*, which should be familiar to the children. However, they should take care when answering the questions as some of the details of the story have been changed. The children can use a dictionary to look up new words and ones they have forgotten. Encourage them first to try to work out the meanings from the sense of the story.

**Developing French
Livre Un
A & C Black**

Picture dictionary

un garçon

une fille

le frère

la sœur

la mère

le père

le
grand-père

la
grand-mère

l'oncle

la tante

le cousin

Developing French
Livre Un
A & C Black

Ma famille

une lettre

une balle

un rideau

du papier

un ballon

la cousine

le bébé

une photographie

un tableau

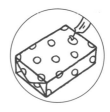
un cadeau

un gâteau

**Developing French
Livre Un
A & C Black**

Recommended resources

Teaching materials

Pilote by Kent Educational Television, 1992–1993, *Pilote plus!,* and *Pilote Moi Interactive by* G. Rumley and K. Sharpe, Kent County Council, 2000 and 2002. Videos, teachers' materials, CD-ROMs and resources for use by non-specialist teachers.

Collins Primary French Starter Pack by Helen Morrison, Collins Educational, 2001. Resource pack of books, posters and audio CDs for non-specialist teachers.

EuroTalk Interactive Learn French from Eurotalk Interactive, 315–317 New Kings Road, London SW6 4RF. CD for PC or Macintosh. An audio CD ideal for beginners.

Workbooks

Mon Album á Moi by Danièle Bourdais and Sue Finney, published by Channel 4 Learning, 2001. Activity book.

Jouons avec Gaston by M. Apicella and H. Challier, published by European Language Institute, 1997. Workbooks with puzzles, games and craft activities.

Speak French and *Speak More French* by Opal Dunn, published by Dorling Kindersley, 1995 and 1997. Packs containing workbooks, activity books, board games and cassettes.

Internet linked French for Beginners by Angela Wilkes, published by Usborne, 2001. Book, audio CD, picture dictionary and puzzle-workbook.

Young Explorers: In France by Jane Ellis, published by Egmont World Limited, 2000. Sticker and activity book.

Dictionaries

First Hundred Words in French by Heather Amery and others, published by Usborne, 1988.

First Thousand Words in French by Heather Amery and others, published by Usborne, 1988.

Larousse MINI Débutants published by Larousse in France, 1985–1986.

Websites

www.bbc.co.uk/education/languages/french

Hear French spoken and test your French using simple games, vocabulary and grammar exercises. There is a specific family section.

www.bonjour.org.uk
French-language puzzles and games.

www.kidscrafty.com
French-language puzzles and games specifically for children, but uses US-English translations.

www.ambafrance-uk.org
French Embassy site with details of French education, culture and information about the country. Links to many other French sites in English and French.

Curriculum information and teaching methods

Modern Foreign Languages: A scheme of work for Key Stage 2 published by Qualifications and Curriculum Authority (QCA) 2000, website: www.nc.uk.net

The Centre for Information on Language Teaching and Research (CILT) has an extensive library of books, audio, video and computer software for teaching French (and other modern foreign languages) at all levels. It produces various information sheets and publications and is the National Advisory Centre on Early Language Learning (NACELL).

Contact or visit CILT at 20 Bedfordbury, London WC2 4LB, tel: 020 7379 5110, e-mail: library@cilt.org.uk, website: http://www.cilt.org.uk

Suppliers of books and teaching materials

Merryman Primary Resources Ltd, PO Box 6718, Bingham, Nottingham, NG13 8QT.
tel: 01949 875 929, e-mail: info@merryman.co.uk, website: www.merryman.co.uk

Bilingual Supplies for Children, PO Box 4081, Bournemouth, Dorset, BH8 9ZZ.
website: www.bilingual-supplies.co.uk

Ecole Alouette, Monkton Road Farm, Birchington, Kent CT7 0JL. tel: 01843 843 447.
e-mail: info@skoldo.com

Early Start Languages, 74 Middle Deal Road, Kent CT14 9RH. tel: 01304 362 569.
e-mail: orders@earlystart.co.uk
website: www.earlystart.co.uk

European Schoolbooks Limited, The Runnings, Cheltenham, Gloucestershire, GL51 9PQ.
tel: 01242 245 252. e-mail: direct@esb.co.uk
websites: www.eurobooks.co.uk

Answers

p 11

Bonjour, je m'appelle Pierre, et toi?
Je m'appelle Marie.
Ça va, Marie?
Oui, ça va, merci.
Au revoir, Marie.
Au revoir, Pierre.

p 12

Je suis un garçon. Je m'appelle Pierre.
Je m'appelle Marie. Je suis une fille.

Comment tu t'appelles?
Je m'appelle Paul.

Je suis un homme.
Je suis une femme.

p 13

Ecoutez!   *Regardez!*
Répétez!   *Taisez-vous!*
Asseyez-vous!   *Levez-vous!*

p 21

quinze et deux font dix-sept
six et sept font treize
neuf et vingt et un font trente
treize et quatorze font vingt-sept
quatre et onze font quinze

14 + 4 = 18
11 + 5 = 16
20 + 6 = 26
13 + 17 = 30
4 + 21 = 25

Et maintenant
Il y a six gommes.
Il y a cinq crayons.
Il y a quatre stylos.

Il y a trois taille-crayons.
Il y a quatre règles.
Il y a deux chaises.

p 22

La fille est sur la boîte.
La fille est devant la boîte.
Le garçon est derrière la fille.

Le garçon est dans la boîte.
Le garçon est devant la fille.
La fille est dans la boîte.

Et maintenant
Le garçon est sur la table.
Le garçon est derrière la chaise.

p 23

Illustrations should show:
a pencil on a table
a ruler in a pencil case
a boy in front of a chair
a rubber behind a pen

Crossword:
Across:
1. trousse
3. taille-crayon
5. garçon
7. gomme
8. fille
Down:
2. stylo
3. table
4. chaise
6. regle

p 24

Je suis un garçon.
J'ai un stylo.

Je suis une fille.
J'ai un crayon.

Je suis un homme.
J'ai un taille-crayon.

Je suis une fille.
J'ai une règle.

Je suis un homme.
J'ai une trousse.

Je suis une femme.
J'ai un stylo.

p 25

The five objects are:
(un) garçon
(un) crayon
(une) gomme
(une) trousse
(une) chaise

p 30

The hidden word is *maison*.

p 34

Crossword:
Across:
1. TOILETTES
2. CANAPE
3. LAVABO
7. LIT
8. REFRIGERATEUR
9. DOUCHE
Down:
1. TABLE
2. CUISINIERE
5. BAIGNOIRE
9. FAUTEUIL

p 35

Sonia est dans la salle de bains.
Pierre est dans la salle à manger.
Fatima est dans la cuisine.
Jamel est dans le salon.
Marie est dans une chambre.
Thierry est dans une chambre.

Et maintenant
(Elle est) dans la salle à manger.
(Il est) dans le salon.

p 36

Sophie:
Je suis derrière la table.
Je suis sur la chaise.
Je suis dans la baignoire.

Joël:
Je suis devant le réfrigérateur.
Je suis dans le fauteuil.
Je suis derrière la cuisinière.

Et maintenant
Possible answers are:
Je suis dans la classe.
Je suis sur une/la chaise.
Je suis derrière une/la table.

p 37
Je suis dans le jardin.
Tu es dans le garage.
Nous sommes dans le jardin.
Ils sont dans la maison.
Vous êtes dans la maison.
Elles sont derrière le mur.
Il est sur le mur. Elle est derrière le mur.

Et maintenant
Il est devant le garage.
Elles sont devant la maison.

p 43
le chat
le canard
le chien
l'oiseau
le mouton
la vache
la poule
le cheval

Et maintenant
miaow
quack, quack
woof, woof
tweet, tweet
baa
moo
cluck, cluck
neigh

p 45
Oui, j'ai un chien.
Non, je n'ai pas de chien.

Oui, j'ai un hamster.
Non, je n'ai pas de hamster.

Oui, j'ai un cheval.
Non, je n'ai pas de cheval.

Oui, j'ai un lapin.
Non, je n'ai pas de lapin.

Oui, j'ai un poisson.
Non, je n'ai pas de poisson.

p 46
Le chat:
Il est dans une chambre.
Il est sur le lit.

Le chien:
Il est dans le salon.
Il est derrière le canapé.

La souris:
Elle est dans une chambre.
Elle est sous le lit.

La vache:
Elle est dans la cuisine.
Elle est devant la cuisinière.

Et maintenant
Le lapin:
Il est dans la salle à manger.
Il est sur la table.

Le cochon:
Il est dans une chambre.
Il est sur le lit.

Le canard:
Il est dans la salle de bains.
Il est dans le lavabo.

p 47

Crossword:
Across:
1. chat
3. cochon
7. poule

9. vache
10. souris
11. lapin
Down:
1. cheval
3. chien
5. poisson
8. oiseau

Et maintenant
un chat
un chien
un cochon
un canard

une vache
un poisson
une poule
un oiseau

un lapin
un mouton
un cheval
une souris

p 52
Top: *Yves, Juliette*
Middle: *Etienne, Emilie*
Bottom: *Thomas, Benjamin, Claire*

p 53
Roger est le grand-père de Sonia.
René est le père de Sonia.
Catherine est la grand-mère de Sonia.
Geneviève est la mère de Sonia.
Paul est le frère de Sonia.
Delphine est la sœur de Sonia.
Sonia est la fille de René.
Paul est le fils de René.

Et maintenant
Possible sentences are:
Delphine est la sœur de Paul.
Robert est le grand-père de Sonia.
Chantal est la grand-mère de Sonia

p 54
C'est Fabien
C'est Alice
C'est David
C'est Sophie
C'est Julie
C'est Karim
C'est Marc
C'est Marie

p 55
The hidden word is *famille*.

p 59
1. In the forest
2. Soup
3. 4 chairs: two big, one medium-sized, one small
4. the medium-sized one
5. Daddy Bear
6. the medium-sized one
7. 'Who has touched my bed?'
8. She ran all the way home.

Et maintenant
un bol	a bowl
une table	a table
une cuillère	a spoon
une chaise	a chair
un lit	a bed